W9-ASB-852

CONTENTS

🌿 Lake Classic Short Stories 🌿

"The universe is made of stories, not atoms."
—Muriel Rukeyser

"The story's about you."
—Horace

Everyone loves a good story. It is hard to think of a friendlier introduction to classic literature. For one thing, short stories are *short*—quick to get into and easy to finish. Of all the literary forms, the short story is the least intimidating and the most approachable.

Great literature is an important part of our human heritage. In the belief that this heritage belongs to everyone, *Lake Classic Short Stories* are adapted for today's readers. Lengthy sentences and paragraphs are shortened. Archaic words are replaced. Modern punctuation and spellings are used. Many of the longer stories are abridged. In all the stories,

5

painstaking care has been taken to preserve the author's unique voice.

Lake Classic Short Stories have something for everyone. The hundreds of stories in the collection cover a broad terrain of themes, story types, and styles. Literary merit was a deciding factor in story selection. But no story was included unless it was as enjoyable as it was instructive. And special priority was given to stories that shine light on the human condition.

Each book in the *Lake Classic Short Stories* is devoted to the work of a single author. Little-known stories of merit are included with famous old favorites. Taken as a whole, the collected authors and stories make up a rich and diverse sampler of the story-teller's art.

Lake Classic Short Stories guarantee a great reading experience. Readers who look for common interests, concerns, and experiences are sure to find them. Readers who bring their own gifts of perception and appreciation to the stories will be doubly rewarded.

❧ John Galsworthy ❧
(1867–1933)

About the Author

John Galsworthy was born into an upper-middle-class English family. He attended the finest schools in England and was trained as a lawyer. But the law was not for him. He once said that he "practiced the law almost not at all, and disliked my profession thoroughly."

Knowing that his son didn't enjoy his work, the elder Galsworthy encouraged the young man to travel. So for nearly two years Galsworthy visited such places as Russia, Canada, Australia, the Fiji Islands, and South Africa.

On one of these voyages, he met the celebrated writer Joseph Conrad. This meeting was the start of a long-lasting friendship. And it marked the beginning of Galsworthy's own interest in a literary career.

In his entire life, Galsworthy seems to have broken the strict rules of conventional British behavior only once. He had a passionate romance with Ada Galsworthy, his cousin's wife. Eventually they ran off together, and were married 10 years later.

Galsworthy's writing is largely a criticism of his own social class. He was always the champion of the rebel, the underdog, and the artist. His most famous work is *The Forsyte Saga*, a series of novels about a British family.

In addition to his novels, Galsworthy wrote several popular plays and collections of short stories. As he grew older, his work lost its sting. His last novels and plays were much more traditional and sentimental than his earlier work.

In 1918, Galsworthy was offered knighthood, but he refused the honor. In 1932, he received the Nobel Prize in Literature.

Quality

Is quality more important than quantity? This is the story of a wonderful boot-maker. Why is his business failing? Does he do his work *too* well?

TO MAKE SUCH BOOTS SEEMED TO ME SOMEHOW
MYSTERIOUS AND WONDERFUL.

Quality

I knew him from the time I was very young. He was my father's boot-maker. The man lived and worked with his older brother. On a small side street, they had turned two little shops into one. Of course, the street is gone now. But in those days it was a most fashionable part of the West End of London.

Their place was special in a quiet way. There was no sign over the door saying that he made boots for any of the Royal Family. There was just his own German name—*Gessler Brothers*. In the window were a few pair of boots. I remember that I always wondered about those boots. For whom had they been made? Usually he made only what was ordered. Had he bought them just to put there? Certainly not! He would never have shown leather that he had not worked himself.

Besides, these boots were too beautiful. The pair of pumps were so very slim. The black leathers with cloth tops were rich enough to make one's mouth water. And the tall brown riding boots had a wonderful glow. Though they were new, they looked as if they could have been worn a hundred years.

Only someone who saw before him the very Soul of Boot could have made them. In them lived the very spirit of all footwear.

These thoughts, of course, came to me when I was older. But even when I was very young, perhaps when I was only about 14, his work amazed me. Even then I had some idea of the greatness of that man and his brother. To make such boots seemed to me then—and still seems to me—somehow mysterious and wonderful.

I remember well my shy question. The day I asked it I was stretching out my young foot to him.

"Isn't it awfully hard to do, Mr. Gessler?"

His answer came with a sudden smile from behind his red beard. "It is an art!"

In looks, he himself seemed made from leather. His face was a crinkly yellow and his hair and beard were a crinkly reddish color. Lines went down his cheeks to the corners of his mouth. His deep, one-toned voice made me think of leather too. Like leather, it was stiff and slow of purpose. His gray-blue eyes were very serious.

His older brother was very like him, but watery and paler in every way. He, too, was a hard worker. Sometimes, in my early days, I was not quite sure which brother was helping me. But I knew when I heard the words, "I will ask my brother." If those words were spoken, I knew I was talking to the older brother.

Sometimes a man grows wilder as he grows older. He might run up bills in the shops. But no one would dream of running up bills with Gessler Brothers. If you owed him money, it would be impossible to stretch out your foot before those blue eyes. And it was not possible to go to him very often. His boots lasted forever. It was like something special was stitched into them.

You went in, not as into most shops, thinking, "Please serve me, and let me go!" No! You went in restfully, as one enters a church. Then, sitting on the one wood chair, you waited. For there was never anybody there. But then he would appear from out of a darkness that smelled of leather. There would be his face, or that of his older brother. Clear blue eyes would be peeking down through iron-rimmed glasses. Then came the tip-tap of slippers beating against the narrow, wood stairs.

Finally, wearing a leather apron and with his sleeves rolled back, he would stand there blinking. Always he seemed as if he had been awakened from a dream of boots. Or perhaps he seemed like an owl surprised and bothered by the daylight.

I would say, "How do you do, Mr. Gessler? Could you make me a pair of Russian boots?"

Without a word he would leave me, going back from where he came. I would continue to rest in the wood chair, breathing the smell of leather. Soon he would come back. A piece of gold-brown leather would be in his worn old hand. With eyes fixed on the leather, he would say, "What a beautiful piece!" He would wait for me to agree. Then he would speak again. "When do you want them?" And I would answer, "Oh! As soon as you can." And he would say, "Two weeks from tomorrow?" Or, if I were talking to his older brother he would say, "I will ask my brother!"

Then I would say, "Thank you! Good morning, Mr. Gessler."

"Good morning!" he would reply, still looking at the leather in his hand. And as I moved to the door, I would hear the tip-tap of his slippers. If I looked around I would see him going back up the stairs to his dream of boots.

It was different if I wanted some new kind of boot that he had not yet made for me. Then, indeed, he would follow a special ceremony. First he would take off my boot and hold it for a long time in his hand. He would look at it carefully and lovingly. It seemed that he was remembering the glow with which he had created it. Then he would place my foot on a piece of paper. Two or three times he would tickle the outside edges of my foot with a pencil. Then he'd pass his fingers over my toes, feeling into the heart of the fit.

I cannot forget a certain day. That was the time I said to him, "Mr. Gessler, that last pair of town walking-boots creaked, you know."

He looked at me for a long time without answering. I felt uncomfortable. It was as if he expected me to take back or change my words. Then he said, "It shouldn't have creaked."

"It did, I'm afraid."

"You got them wet before they were broken in?"

"I don't think so."

At that he lowered his eyes as if trying to remember the boots. I wished I had not said anything at all.

"Send them back!" he said. "I will look at them."

Suddenly I felt sorry for my poor, creaking boots. I could imagine the sorrowful long looks he would give them.

"Some boots," he said slowly, "are bad from birth. If I can do nothing with them, I will take them off your bill."

Once—only once—I forgot what I was doing. I went into his shop wearing a pair of boots that I had bought quickly from a larger store. He took my order without showing me any leather. I could feel his eyes on my feet.

"Those are not my boots."

The tone was not one of anger nor of sorrow. But there was something quiet in it that made the blood run cold. Then he put his hand down. He pressed a finger on the place where the left boot was not quite comfortable.

"It hurts you there," he said. "Those big stores don't care!" And then, as if something had given out in him, he spoke long and bitterly. It was the only time I ever heard him talk about the problems of his trade.

"They get it all," he said. "They get customers by advertising, not by work. They take it away from us, who love our boots. It comes to this—pretty soon I will have no work. Every year it gets less. You will see." Looking at his lined face, I saw things I had never noticed before. I saw bitter things and hard struggle. And what a lot of gray hairs there suddenly seemed to be in his red beard!

As best I could, I explained why I had these other boots. But his face and voice got to me! During the next few minutes

I ordered many pairs. But, wouldn't you know, these new boots lasted longer than ever! I was not able to return to him for nearly two years.

When at last I went back, I was surprised to find that something had changed. Outside one of the two little windows of his shop, another name was painted. It was also the name of a boot-maker. Of course, the sign announced that the man made boots for the Royal Family. The old, familiar boots were no longer spread across the front windows. Now they were pushed together in just one window.

Inside the one little shop, the smell of leather was stronger. It was darker than ever. And my wait was longer than usual, too. It seemed to take forever before a face peeked down and the tip-tap of the slippers began. At last he stood before me. Looking through his rusty iron glasses, he said, "Ah, it's you, isn't it?"

"Ah! Mr. Gessler," I stammered, "but your boots are really *too* good, you know! See, these are quite nice still!" And I stretched out my foot to him. He looked at it.

"Yes," he said. "These days people do not want good boots, it seems."

Not knowing how to reply, I quickly said, "What have you done to your shop?"

He answered quietly. "It was too costly. Do you want some boots?"

I ordered three pairs, though I had only wanted two. Then I quickly left. In his mind, I feared that I was part of a plot against him. Or if not against *him*, against his idea of boot. I suppose I did not care to feel like that, for it was again many months before my next visit to his shop. Then, I remember thinking, "Oh, well! I can't leave the old boy. So, here goes! Perhaps it will be his older brother!"

For his older brother, I knew, did not

have as strong a character. I knew he would not scold me, even with a silent look.

And, indeed, in the shop there appeared to be his older brother.

"Well, Mr. Gessler," I said, "how are you?"

He came nearer and looked at me closely.

"I am pretty well," he said slowly. "But my older brother is dead."

And I saw that it was indeed himself. But how aged and pale he was! And never before had I heard him speak of his brother. Much surprised, I whispered, "Oh! I am sorry!"

"Yes," he answered. "He was a good man. He made a good boot. But he is dead." He shook his head. His hair had gone as thin as his poor brother's. "He could not get over losing the other shop. Do you want any boots?" He held up a fine piece of leather in his hand. "It's a beautiful piece."

I ordered several pairs. It was very long before they came, but they were better than ever. One simply could not wear them out. And soon after that, I went on a long trip.

It was over a year before I was again in London. The first shop I went to was my old friend's. I had left a man of sixty. When I came back, he looked seventy-five. He was thin and worn and shaky. At first he did not know me.

"Oh! Mr. Gessler," I said, sick at heart, "how wonderful your boots are! See, I have been wearing this pair nearly all the time I've been away. They are not half worn out, are they?"

He looked long at my boots, a pair made of Russian leather. His face seemed to brighten. Putting his hand on my foot, he said, "Do they fit you here? I had trouble with that pair, I remember."

I told him that they fit beautifully.

"Do you want any boots?" he said. "I can make them quickly. Things are slow now."

I answered, "Please, please! I want lots of boots, every kind!"

"I will make a fresh model. Your foot must be bigger." And very slowly he drew a pencil around my foot. He felt my toes. He looked up only once to say, "Did I tell you my brother was dead?"

He had grown so weak that it hurt to watch him. I was glad to get away.

I had nearly forgotten I had ordered those boots. Then one evening they came. Opening the box, I set the four pairs out in a row. Then one by one, I tried them on. There was no doubt about it. These boots fit better and felt better than any he had ever made me. Tucked into one of the boots, I found his bill. The amount was the same as usual—but it surprised me. He had never before sent the bill until weeks after he sent the boots. I flew down the stairs and wrote a check. I mailed it at once.

A week later I passed the little street. I thought I would go in and tell him how wonderfully the new boots fit. But when I came to his shop, I saw that his name was gone. In the window were still the pair of pumps, the black leathers with cloth tops, and the tall brown riding boots.

I went in, very much worried. The two little shops had been again made into one. There stood a young man with an English face.

"Mr. Gessler in?" I asked.

He gave me a strange look.

"No, sir," he said, "no. But we can help you with anything you need. We have taken the shop over. You saw our name, no doubt, next door. We make boots for some very good people."

"Yes, yes," I said, "but Mr. Gessler?"

"Oh!" he answered. "He is dead."

"Dead! But I only received these boots from him last week."

"Ah!" he said. "It was a shocking thing. Poor old man starved himself."

"Good heavens!"

"Slowly starved, the doctor told us. You see he went to work in such a way! He would keep the shop going no matter what. He wouldn't let anyone touch his boots except himself. When he got an order, it took him such a long time. People won't wait. He lost everybody.

"But there he would sit, working on and on. I will say this for him—not a man in London made a better boot! But there were so many other shops. And he never advertised! He would have only the best leather too, no matter what it cost. Well, there it is. What could you expect with his old-fashioned ideas?"

"But to starve!"

"That may be a bit strong. But I know myself that he was sitting over his boots day and night to the very end. You see, I used to watch him. He never gave himself time to eat. He never had a penny in the house. All his money went into rent and leather. How he lived so long, I don't know. I think he just let his fire go out. He was a character. But he made good boots."

"Yes," I said, "he made good boots."

The Pack

Do individuals change when they act as a group? In this revealing story, a man shares a shameful memory from his schooldays. What does his story say about human nature?

CHALKCROFT DIDN'T FIT IN WITH THE REST OF THE
FELLOWS. PROBABLY HE HAD NEVER FIT ANYWHERE IN
HIS LIFE.

The Pack

"It's only when men run in packs," said H., "that they lose their sense of right and wrong. At least that's what life has shown me. A man alone is more given to kindness than meanness. Alone, he is seldom cruel. He leans, in fact, towards being a gentleman.

"The trouble comes when you add three or four more to him. It is then that his sense of right and wrong—of what he should or shouldn't do—goes out the window.

"I am not at all sure that it is much different than catching a fever. Something takes place inside his body, I fancy. I happen to do some work in a group with three others. When we get together, we can be pretty tight with money. We cut some corners and pinch pennies in a way that each of us, alone, would never dream of."

"On the whole," said D., "I quite agree. Single man is not an angel. But man as a part of a group is a bit of an animal."

The talk was carried on for several minutes. Then P., who had been silent, spoke up. "I have an example that is better than hours of talk," he said. "When I was in college, there was a young man with me called Chalkcroft. He was a perfectly sweet, well-mannered fellow. He had some very different ideas, of course. Some people even thought he was a Socialist.

"Anyway, he wore an odd turn-down collar and a silly green tie, and he never joined us in any of the college fun. He just didn't fit in with the rest of the fellows. Probably he had never fit in anywhere in his life. He played no games that used a ball, and he was afraid of horses and women.

"Chalkcroft liked to take long, lonely walks or row a boat alone on the river. He also read books all the time. For all these reasons, he was looked down upon by almost every self-respecting student.

"Don't imagine, of course, that his case was unusual. We had many such odd ducks at school in my time. But this Chalkcroft seemed to be comfortable, and quietly sure of himself. He was thought to be a "bit above himself." In truth, he did not seem to realize that he was a bit below his fellows.

"On the contrary, his slim, slightly

stooping figure passed about the college peacefully. His pale face, with its shadow of whisker, always wore a little smile above his hated green tie. And he could not even use poverty as an excuse for his strangeness. He was *not* poor. In fact he had some of the best rooms in college."

"For these reasons," P. went on, "it was decided one evening to bring him to trial. This was the bright idea of a third-year man named Jefferies. He was a dark person with an elephant-like nose and walk. He had a biting, clever tongue, and very small eyes. Now he is a member of Scottish royalty. This young gentleman could be quite mean.

"Jefferies was interested in law. It was his practice to enter the rooms of any person whom he believed deserved a trial. Once there, he would hold that trial with all the ceremony of the British courts. I had gone to one of these trials before. The man being tried was a chuckle-headed young fellow whose jokes were really terrible. The ceremony was funny enough, and the fellow did not seem to mind. He grinned from ear to ear and cried, "Oh! I say, Jefferies!"

"Chalkcroft's trial was a different sort of thing altogether. We found the man at home. He was reading before his fire by the light of three candles. The yellow candle flames barely lit up the darkness as we came laughing in.

"'Chalkcroft,' said Jefferies, 'we are going to try you.' Chalkcroft stood up and looked at us. He was wearing a jacket and his usual green tie. His face was a bit pale.

"He answered, 'Yes, Jefferies? You forgot to knock.'

"Jefferies put out his finger and thumb. He quickly pulled Chalkcroft's tie from out of the jacket.

"'You wear a green tie, sir,' he said.

"Chalkcroft went as gray as the ashes in the fireplace. Then, slowly, a white-hot glow came into his cheeks.

"'Don't look at me, sir,' said Jefferies. 'Look at the jury!' He waved his hand at us. 'We are going to try you for—' He described some terrible act. It was the same one that served as the charge for most of his trials.

"We laughed and laughed. Then we settled ourselves in chairs. Jefferies sat himself on a table and slowly crossed his thin legs. His little black eyes looked bright and mean above his huge nose. Chalkcroft was still standing.

"It was then," said P., "that I first began to worry. The fellow was so still and pale. He looked at me. But when I tried to look back, his eyes passed me over. He was very quiet and calm. It wasn't natural. I remember thinking,

'Why are we all here? We are not a bit the kind of men to do this sort of thing.' And really we were not—except for Jefferies. He, no doubt, was taken over by a devil from time to time.

"Perhaps I should include Anderson along with Jefferies. Anderson was a little man with a red nose and very long arms. I believe that he has since become a school teacher. Besides Jefferies and Anderson, we were all decent fellows. Left to himself, not a one of us would have entered another man's rooms without being asked. No matter how unpopular a man might be, none of us would have insulted him to his face.

"There was Beal, a rather good-looking man, who was very fair and honest. There was Dunsdayle, a heavy, long-faced person. He liked a good time, but he never did anything really wrong. And there was Horden, a big, clean-cut fellow with nice eyes and fists like hammers.

"Stickland was fussy but kind. Sevenoax is now in government, in the house of Lords. And my old school friend Fosdyke was far above such stuff. We had all, or nearly all, come from the 'best' schools in the country. Now we were in the 'best' set at college. Alone, each and every one of us was a gentleman.

"Jefferies picked Anderson to be the jailer. Dunsdale was to present the case. The rest of us were the jury. Jefferies, himself, was judge. He was, as I have said, a clever young man. Swinging his legs and keeping his black eyes on Chalkcroft, he moved things right along.

"I have forgotten just exactly what happened during the trial. But, as if he were standing here before us, I can still remember Chalkcroft's pale, still face. I can still see it in the dim light of those three candles. I remember his repeated

'Yes, Jefferies.' And I remember his one question, *'Are you a gentleman, Jefferies?'*

"We laughed madly at that. As if he were standing right here before us, I remember the look on his face. And I can still hear Jefferies' final question. 'Prisoner, are you guilty? Yes or no?' There came a long, silent moment. Then Chalkcroft's answer, slow and cutting, 'As you like, Jefferies.'

"As if he were standing here before us, I remember his calm. He hated us and he was above us. His sentence was to drink a glass of his own wine without stopping. Whether the sentence was carried out, I cannot tell you. Along with one or two more, I slipped away.

"The next morning I felt very uncomfortable. I could not rest until I had sent Chalkcroft a letter saying how sorry I was. That afternoon I caught sight of him walking across the yard. His face wore its usual pale calm. In the evening I received his answer. It ended with this sentence, 'I feel sure you would not have come if it hadn't been for the others.'

"It has crossed my mind since that he may have said the same thing to us all. For all I know, we may all have written."

There was a silence. Then H. said, "The Pack? Ah! What devil is it that gets into us when we run in packs?"

The Meeting

Can you tell much about strangers just by watching them? In this insightful story, a man notices a young couple in a teahouse. What he observes about their meeting may surprise you.

I KNEW THAT THIS WAS THEIR FIRST STOLEN MEETING.

The Meeting

I was walking one day in Kensington Gardens. By chance I strolled into an outdoor teahouse. I sat down on the side that was protected from the east wind. This was the side where the fashionable people never go.

New leaves were swinging in a breeze. The wind kept stealing up in puffs under the half-bare branches. Birds hunted in the grass for crumbs. Most of the cream-colored chairs and little round-topped tables were empty. They seemed to be sending out lonely invitations to come and sit down.

A few of these tables were taken. At one sat a pale, thin child in a large white hat. She was with a cheery nurse and an older lady in gray. The older woman looked as if she were fighting some long sickness. At another table, two ladies—Americans, perhaps—were eating rolls. They had pleasant, tanned faces. At a third table, a bald, square man sat smoking. Now and then, like the cry of the very heart of spring, came the scream of peacocks from across the grass.

Before long a young man came strolling along the path. He wore a fine cut-away coat, a shining top hat, and black boots. Nervously, he was swinging a cane. His face was fresh and his color was high. He had a little twisted dark mustache and bold, bright eyes. I noticed that the man walked like an athlete. His legs were hard with muscle.

The young man looked about him as if he didn't care about a thing. But under his careless look, I saw that he was waiting, expecting, worrying. He passed by again. Certainly he was looking for someone. Then I lost sight of him for a moment.

But soon he came back. This time he had *her* with him. Oh! She was pretty, with her veil and her flower-like face behind it. She looked quickly from left to right, while putting on an air of perfect ease. And yet, there was a hint of many feelings behind that air. Perhaps there was a bit of unhappiness about where she was, a wicked satisfaction, a hope not to be caught. And he? How changed he was! His eyes were no longer uneasy. Now they were full of delight and worship. The careless look was gone.

He picked a table not far from mine. It was quite well-hidden from most of the others. He drew her chair back for her, and down they sat. I could not hear their talk, but I could watch them. As if they had told me in so many words, I knew that this was their first stolen meeting. The important thing was that *they must not be seen.*

Or perhaps, it was the first meeting that they *felt* must not be seen. The two were very different things. In their own minds, they had stepped over the line that divided what people should and should not do. Perhaps this moment had been months in coming. It was the moment of beginning that in each love affair comes only once. It was the moment that makes the sweet pain ahead so easy to bear.

Their eyes told the whole story. Hers restlessly looked all around, and then suddenly clung to his. His eyes tried to show calm—but they showed only that he belonged to her. It was interesting to watch the difference between the woman and the man. In the middle of their stolen joy, she had her eye on the world. She cared what people thought. It seemed clear to her that she was in the wrong. But his worries about the world's opinions had gone by the board. All he cared about was that he was looking into her eyes.

"Forget the world!" he said to himself. But she still watched the world as a cat carefully watches a big dog. When their eyes met, however, they could not for a moment tear themselves apart. Watching them gave me an ache in the heart. It was the same ache that the cry of the peacock brings. Or the first spring scent of the flowering trees.

I began wondering. Their love had a life. It was just now flowering like the trees. It would bud, blossom, and die. Were these unusual people? Not they!

They were just a pair of lovers, this man and woman. They were clean, and bright, and young. Spring was in their blood.

Both of them were fresh-run, as they say of the salmon. And they were as certain as the salmon to drift back to the sea when their time was up. The couple bent their heads together. To them, all rights and wrongs and warnings of tomorrow didn't matter. Nothing would stop them—no more than an icy shower would stop the march of spring.

I thought of what was in store. For him, there would be hours of waiting, with his heart in his mouth. He would not know whether she would come, or why she did not come. For her, there would be the hours of wondering. "Does he really love me? He cannot really love me!" There would be stolen meetings and happiness that disappears at the thought of parting.

Then would come the actual partings themselves, the emptiness in the heart, and the beginning of waiting again. She would wait for secret letters and make excuses for going out. He would pass her house after dark to see the lights in the windows. Then he would try to judge what was really going on. There would be jealousy and fear and hours of hard walking to drive away the fit. He would spend sleepless nights, wanting her.

And then the fatal hour would come. Perhaps it would come on some stolen day on the river, or under the cover of a wood. That face of hers on the trip home would lead him to offer to kill himself. Anything to save her from his presence! Then would come a promise to meet once more. There would be fierce delights. But always underneath, like the deepest notes of a song, would be the endless lies and secrets.

And then, the slow process of cooling starts. Then the beginning of excuses. "I'm sorry," they will say, but they will start to find things wrong in each other. And finally there is the day when she does not come, or he does not come. And then the letters begin, the sudden stiff manners, and the still more sudden— end.

It all came before my mind, like the scenes of a movie. But under the table I saw their hands join together. The pictures of the future disappeared. Wisdom, knowledge, and all the rest— what were they to that tender touch!

So, getting up, I left them there. I walked away under the trees, with the cry of the peacock following.

Virtue

She was so pretty and innocent-looking! Harold Mellesh was only trying to help the poor girl. How could a good deed cause him so much trouble?

"HERE," HE SAID. "I'LL PAY HER FINE."

Virtue

Harold Mellesh worked as a clerk in
an accident insurance company. One day
his job took him to a certain police court
to go over the matter of a smashed car.
There he stood watching the workings of
the law. His eyes were blue and rather
like those of a baby. Today they were
opened very wide. His forehead was so
wrinkled that it moved the curly hair on
his head. His hands tightened around
the straw hat that he held at his chest.

Harold Mellesh had just seen four

ladies of the streets brought before the court. Three were jailed. One was fined. The last lady to appear caught his special attention. Perhaps she was prettier than the others. Certainly she was younger, and she was crying.

"First time you've been here—two pounds and ten shillings fine."

"But I haven't any money, sir."

"Very well—14 days."

Tears streaked the powder on her face. She made a strange little sound. Feelings bubbled up in young Mellesh, like a kettle coming to a boil. He touched a blue sleeve in front of him.

"Here," he said. "I'll pay her fine."

He felt the policeman's look run over him like a bug.

"Friend of yours?"

"No."

"I wouldn't, then. She'll be back here again within the month."

The girl was passing. He saw that she

was swallowing her tears. "I don't care. I'll pay," he said.

The policeman stared at him coldly.

"Come with me, then."

Young Mellesh followed him out.

"Here," said the policeman to the guard in charge of the girl. "This gentleman will pay the fine."

The girl looked confused. Young Mellesh's own cheeks turned bright red. He brought out his money and found that he only had two pounds and fifteen shillings. He handed over the two pounds, ten shillings. "My word!" he thought. "What would Alice say?"

He heard the girl gasp out, "Oh! Thank you!"

The policeman muttered, "Waste of money! Still, it was a kind act."

Young Mellesh then went out into the street. His feelings had given off two pounds, ten shillings worth of steam. Now he felt cold and dizzy. It was as if

the virtue had gone out of him. Then a
voice behind him said, "Thank you ever
so much. That *was* kind of you."

He lifted his straw hat and stood aside
to let the girl pass.

She pushed a card into his hand. "Any
time you are passing, I'll be glad to see
you. I'm very grateful."

"Not at all!" His smile was as confused
as her own. But he had to get back to his
office. He turned away and hurried down
the street.

All day long he felt uncertain. Had he
been a fool? Had he been a hero?
Sometimes he thought, "What animals
they are to those girls!" And sometimes
he thought, "I don't know. I suppose the
police must do something about it." And
he tried not to think about Alice. How
would he explain the loss of two pounds
and ten shillings? He knew that Alice
had been counting on that money.

That night he reached home at 6:30,

his usual hour. His house was gray and small and had just a bit of green grass all around. His wife had just put their baby daughter to bed. Just now she was sitting in her chair, sewing up the holes in his socks. She looked up as he came in. Upon seeing her, Mellesh noticed with surprise how very much her forehead looked like a knee.

"There's something wrong with the way you wear your socks, Harold," she said. "It's all I can do to sew up this pair."

Her eyes were china-blue and as round as plates. Her voice had but one tone. She had been brought up to show little of her feelings. She was a farmer's daughter, and young Mellesh had become engaged to her while on a holiday. Now he noticed how pale she looked, even though he himself was a bit pale from the office and the heat.

"The heat is terrible, isn't it?" she said. "Sometimes I wish we'd never had baby.

It does tie you down in the evenings. I *am* looking forward to our holiday, that I am."

Young Mellesh, tall and thin, bent over and kissed her forehead. How on earth could he let her know that he had blown their holiday? He was just now seeing that he had done an awful thing.

Perhaps.... Oh! Surely she would understand how he *had* to do what he did. He couldn't see that girl being jailed just because she was short of a few pounds. But he didn't mention the girl until the end of their small supper.

"I got quite upset this morning, Alice," he said suddenly. "I had to go down to the police court about that car smash I told you about. Afterwards, I saw them run in a lot of those street girls from Piccadilly. It made me sick to see the way they treat them."

His wife looked up. Her face was like a child's.

"Why? What do they do to them?"

"Jail them for speaking to men in the street."

"I suppose they're up to no good."

The matter-of-fact tone of her voice bothered young Mellesh. But he went on bravely.

"They speak to them as if they were dirt."

"Well—aren't they?"

"Oh, they may be a loose lot, but so are men."

"Men wouldn't be so loose if it weren't for those women."

"I suppose it's all a big circle." Then he added, "One or two of them were pretty."

His wife smiled. Her smile had a comfortable, teasing look about it.

"They treat the pretty ones better, I suppose?"

Then he let it all out. "One girl was quite young. She had never been there before. They were going to throw her in jail just because she hadn't any money! I couldn't put up with it. I paid her fine."

There was sweat on his forehead. His wife's face was turning quite pink.

"*You* paid? How much?"

He was on the point of saying, "Ten shillings." But something deep inside him pushed for the truth. "Two pounds, ten shillings," he said. Then he thought unhappily, "Oh! What a fool I've been!"

He did wish that Alice wouldn't open her mouth like that when nothing was coming out. It made her look so silly! Then suddenly her face became quite blank. He felt guilty and ashamed—as if he had hit her.

"Awfully sorry, Alice," he whispered. "I never meant to. She—she cried."

"Of course she cried! You fool, Harold!"

He got up. He was very upset.

"Well, and what would *you* have done?" he asked.

"Me? Let her stew in her own juice, of course. It wasn't your problem."

She too had gotten to her feet. He pulled his fingers through his hair. In his mind, he could see the girl's face, tear-streaked, confused, and very pretty. He could hear her soft, common, grateful voice. His wife turned her back. So! He was in for a fit of silence. Well! No doubt he had earned it.

"I dare say, I *was* a fool," he muttered. "But I did have a hope that you would understand! You can imagine how I felt when I saw her cry. Suppose it had been *you* in her place!" From the toss of her head, he knew he had said something very wrong.

"Oh! So that's what you think of me!" she said.

He touched her shoulder. "Of course I don't, Alice. Don't be silly!"

She shook off his hand. "Whose money

was it? Now baby and I will get no holiday. And all because you see a fast and easy street-girl, crying."

Before he could answer, she was gone. He had an awful sense that he had done a terrible wrong. He had given away her holiday! Given his wife's holiday to a girl of the streets! Still, it was his own holiday, too. Besides, he had earned the money! He'd never wanted to give it to the girl. He hadn't got anything for it! Suppose he had put it into the offering plate at church? Then, would Alice have been so angry—even if it was all of their holiday money? He didn't see much difference.

He sat down and planted his elbows on his knees. He stared at the flowers on the carpet. They still owed money on that carpet. All those feelings that rise in people who live together— when they don't agree—swirled in his curly head. His eyes showed his feelings, just like a

baby's. They *did* treat those poor girls
like dirt! If only she hadn't cried! She
hadn't meant to cry. He could tell that
by the sound of it. And who was that
judge, anyway? Who was any man to
treat her like that?

Alice shouldn't.... But suddenly he
pictured Alice again, bending over his
socks. She was pale and tired with the
heat. All day long she had been doing
things for him or the baby. And he had
given away her holiday! No getting
around that. Oh, he was sorry for what
he had done. He must go up and try to
make his peace. He would sell his bicycle.
She should have her holiday after all.
Oh, yes—they all should!

He opened the door and listened. The
little house was very quiet. The only
sounds came from the outside. He heard
buses passing on the road and children
playing on doorsteps. She must be up in
the bedroom with the baby!

He climbed the steep, white-washed stairway. It needed a carpet and fresh paint. Ah! There were a lot of other things Alice wanted. You couldn't have everything at once on four pounds, ten shillings a week! But she should have remembered there were things that he wanted too—yes, and badly. And he never thought of getting them. The door of their bedroom was locked. He shook the handle. Then she opened it suddenly, and stood facing him on the little landing.

"I don't want you up here."

"Look here, Alice. This is rotten."

She stepped out on the landing and closed the door behind her.

"It is! You go downstairs again. I don't want you. Do you think I believe that— about the girl crying? I'd be ashamed, if I were you!"

Ashamed! He might have been too soft-hearted. But why should he be ashamed?

"You think I don't know what men are like?" she went on. "You can go back to your rotten girl, if she is so pretty!" She stood straight and stiff against the door. Red spots flamed in her cheeks. She seemed so sure of herself that she almost made him feel like a villain.

"Alice! Good heavens! You must be crazy! I've done nothing wrong!"

"But you would *like* to. Go along! I don't want you!" He was taken back by the sharp look of her blue eyes and the force of her voice. The bitter line of her mouth made him feel—well, that he knew nothing about anything. He leaned back against the wall.

"Well, I'll be darned!" was all he could get out.

"Do you mean to say she didn't ask you back to her room?"

The palms of his hands grew wet. The

girl's card was in his pocket!

"Well, if the cat has got your tongue, I can't help it. What do you think I am? Giving your own child's money to a dirty little street girl! You owed it to us—that's the truth. Go on with you! Don't stand there!"

He had a sudden longing to hit her on the mouth. It looked so bitter. "Well," he said slowly, "now I understand."

But what was it that he understood? That she was hard and stiff and came down sharp on people?

"I thought—I think you might—" he whispered.

"Ugh!" she exclaimed. The sound was so ugly that he turned to go downstairs.

"You have buried us, you white beast!" she cried.

The door clicked before he could answer her strange words. He heard the key turn. Idiot! The little landing seemed

too small to hold his feelings. Would he
have said a word to Alice if he had done
anything wrong with the girl? Why, he
had never even thought of doing
anything!

Confused, he ran down the stairs. He
pulled his straw hat from the rack and
went out. The streets smelled of London
fog, fried fish, gasoline, and hot, dirty
people. Feeling very troubled, he walked
along. His eyes were sad. So this was
what he was really married to—this—
this! It was like being married to that
police court! It wasn't human to have so
little trust. What was the use of being
kind and honest if this was all a man got
for it?

"Mister, you're all white behind. Let
me brush you."

He stood still, feeling very confused. A
large, fair man dusted his back up and
down with a big flat hand. *White beast!*

He must have leaned up against the white-washed wall on the stairway. A bubble of rage rose to his lips. All right, then!

He felt in his pocket for the girl's card. Then he was suddenly surprised to find that he had no need to look for it. He remembered the address. It was not far off, just on the other side of the Euston Road. Had he been looking at the card without knowing it? He wasn't sure. But he did know that he was going to get even with Alice!

He reached the Euston Road. Crossing it, he began to feel a strange, pleasant weakness in his legs. By this time he knew that he was going to do wrong. He was not going to visit the girl just to get even with his wife, but because he expected to . . . ! That was bad, bad. It would put Alice in the right!

He stood still at a corner garden with

railings around it. He leaned against one of the railings. His eyes searched the trees. He had always been quite honest with his wife. It was she who had put the idea into his head. And yet his legs, being pleasantly weak, seemed in some way to say that she was right.

Harold Mellesh wasn't sure what to do. It was just like he had felt at the police court. Without Alice, without the police court, where would he be? Where would any man be? Without virtue! Completely without virtue! A bird in the garden sang.

"Anytime you're passing, I'll be glad to see you," the girl had said. Her voice had sounded honest, really grateful. And the girl had looked—not worse than anybody else! If only Alice had looked at his side of it all! He would never have thought of the girl again. That is, unless—well!

The doubt made his legs move forward.

He was a married man. That was all there was to it. But he looked across at the numbers on the houses. Yes, there it was—number 27! A flowering branch brushed his face. The sweet smell made him think of the days when he and Alice were courting. The real Alice—not the Alice on the landing!

As he looked closely at the shabby house, he suddenly went hot all over. Suppose he went in there. What would that girl think? That he had a purpose in mind for paying her fine. But that wasn't it at all. Oh, no! He wasn't that kind of man! He turned his face away and walked on, fast and far.

The signs above the theaters were lit. There were very few cars on the streets. The only people in sight moved about slowly. Harold Mellesh came to the square and sat down on a bench. In the dusk, the street lamps and the theater lights around him grew slowly brighter. Sitting there, he thought about how sad life is. There was so much of everything— but one got so little of anything!

Harold Mellesh added up figures all day, and then went home to Alice. That was life! Well, it wasn't so bad when Alice was nice to him. But, oh, what one missed! The books about the South Sea Islands—places, peoples, sights, sounds, smells, all over the world! Four pounds and ten shillings a week, a wife, a baby! Well, you couldn't have life both ways. But had he got them *either* way? Not with the Alice on the landing!

Ah! Well! Poor Alice! Jolly hard on her to miss her holiday! But she might have given him a chance to tell her that he would sell his bicycle. Or was it all a bad dream? Had he ever really been in that police court? Had he really seen them sending those girls off to prison? And

weren't those girls a lot like himself—
people who had missed too much? The
police would catch a fresh lot of them
tonight. What a fool he had been to pay
that fine!

"Glad I didn't go along to that girl's
house, anyway," he thought. "I would
have felt like a scum!" There had been
only one good thing about it: the look on
her face when she said, "Oh! Thank you!"
Even now, remembering that look gave
him a warm feeling.

But then that feeling, too, turned cold.
Nothing for it! When he had finished
sitting there, he must go home! If Alice
had thought him wrong before—what
would she think when he returned? Well,
there it was! The milk had been spilled!
But he did wish that Alice didn't have
such a virtue about her.

The sky deepened and darkened. The
lights were bright and white. The flower
beds in the square seemed cut out and

stiff, like the sets on a stage. He must go back and face it! No good to worry!

Harold Mellesh got up from the bench and gave himself a shake. Turned towards the lights of the hills, his eyes were round, honest, and good, like the eyes of a baby.

Thinking About
the Stories

Quality

1. Good writing always has an effect on the reader. How did you feel when you finished reading this story? Were you surprised, horrified, amused, sad, touched, or inspired? What elements in the story made you feel that way?

2. What period of time is covered in this story—an hour, a week, several years? What role, if any, does time play in the story?

3. Which character in this story do you most admire? Why? Which character do you like the least?

The Pack

1. Many stories are meant to teach a lesson of some kind. Is the author trying to make a point in this story? What is it?

2. What is the title of this story? Can you think of another good title?

3. Is there a character in this story who makes you think of yourself or someone you know? What did the character say or do to make you think that?

The Meeting

1. Look back at the illustration that introduces this story. What character or characters are pictured? What is happening in the scene? What clues does the picture give you about the time and place of the story?

2. Some stories are packed with action. In other stories, the key events take place in the minds of the characters. Is this story told more through the characters' thoughts and feelings? Or is it told more through their outward actions?

3. Compare and contrast at least two characters in this story. In what ways are they alike? In what ways are they different?

Virtue

1. All the events in a story are arranged in a certain order, or sequence. Tell about one event from the beginning of this story, one from the middle, and one from the end. How are these events related?

2. All stories fit into one or more categories. Is this story serious or funny? Would you call it an adventure, a love story, or a mystery? Is it a character study? Or is it simply a picture the author has painted of a certain time and place? Explain your thinking.

3. The plot is the series of events that takes place in a story. Usually, story events are linked in some way. Can you name an event in this story that was the cause of a later event?

Thinking About
the Book

1. Choose your favorite illustration in this book. Use this picture as a springboard to write a new story. Give the characters different names. Begin your story with something they are saying or thinking.

2. Compare the stories in this book. Which was the most interesting? Why? In what ways were they alike? In what ways different?

3. Good writers usually write about what they know best. If you wrote a story, what kind of characters would you create? What would be the setting?

LAKE CLASSICS

Great American Short Stories I

Washington Irving, Nathaniel Hawthorne, Mark Twain, Bret Harte, Edgar Allan Poe, Kate Chopin, Willa Cather, Sarah Orne Jewett, Sherwood Anderson, Charles W. Chesnutt

Great American Short Stories II

Herman Melville, Stephen Crane, Ambrose Bierce, Jack London, Edith Wharton, Charlotte Perkins Gilman, Frank R. Stockton, Hamlin Garland, O. Henry, Richard Harding Davis

Great British and Irish Short Stories I

Arthur Conan Doyle, Saki (H. H. Munro), Rudyard Kipling, Katherine Mansfield, Thomas Hardy, E. M. Forster, Robert Louis Stevenson, H. G. Wells, John Galsworthy, James Joyce

Great Short Stories from Around the World I

Guy de Maupassant, Anton Chekhov, Leo Tolstoy, Selma Lagerlöf, Alphonse Daudet, Mori Ogwai, Leopoldo Alas, Rabindranath Tagore, Fyodor Dostoevsky, Honoré de Balzac

Cover and Text Designer: Diann Abbott

Library of Congress Catalog Number: 94-075359
ISBN 1-56103-034-1
Printed in the United States of America
1 9 8 7 6 5 4 3 2

LAKE CLASSICS

*Great British and Irish
Short Stories I*

John
GALSWORTHY

Stories retold by Joanne Suter
Illustrated by James McConnell

LAKE EDUCATION
Belmont, California